Could do
better

Could do better

Collected by Patrick Dickinson

Illustrated by David English

*A royalty on each copy of this book
will be paid to the
Save the Children Fund*

ARROW BOOKS

Arrow Books Limited
17–21 Conway Street, London W1P 6JD

An imprint of the Hutchinson Publishing Group

London Melbourne Sydney Auckland
Johannesburg and agencies throughout
the world

First published 1982
© Patrick Dickinson 1982

Set in Linotron Bembo
by Rowland Phototypesetting Limited
Bury St Edmunds, Suffolk

Made and printed in Great Britain
by The Anchor Press Ltd
Tiptree, Essex

ISBN 0 09 928320 4

Foreword

In one of my school reports a perceptive Form Master wrote: 'Where work is concerned, Patrick is happy to leave most of it to others.'

If he were to stumble upon this book, he would see how little I've changed. Indeed, I don't mind admitting that I'm more than happy to leave the writing of the book to the celebrated contributors who have responded so willingly and so generously with quotations and encouraging letters. The warmth of their response has made the whole enterprise a most rewarding experience.

My only regret is that we have not been able to fit into a book of this size all the quotations and comments that were sent to me.

I work with children in a social priority area on Tyneside. The idea of doing something to help the work of the Save the Children Fund came to me one day in 1980. A documentary film on television showed a team of British doctors and nurses working in a remote area of Southeast Asia. They were trying to share a tiny supply of medicines and food among hundreds of sick and starving children. It was obvious that the supply was hopelessly inadequate. Now, two years later, I'd like to think that the sale of this book might help the Save the Children Fund to make life a little better for those children I saw and for many others. I'm delighted to say that all the royalties are being donated to the Save the Children Fund.

May I express my thanks to the many people who have helped me with this book:

First of all, to the many celebrities for their contributions in words and pictures;

To the publishers for increasing the royalty that is being donated to the Save the Children Fund;

To the Argyle Printing Company in Newcastle for printing the 350 letters – and the 100 reminder cards I sent out!

Finally, let me say thank you to you for buying a copy of the book, and for not merely 'leaving it to others'. . . .

Patrick Dickinson

MAX BYGRAVES

My headmaster wrote: 'Bygraves is a carbuncle on the backside of humanity and will never be a success.' I saw him a few weeks ago in Piccadilly – I was in my Rolls-Royce. I got the chauffeur to stop, I walked back to where he was standing in the gutter and I kicked his tray of matches in the air.

Max Bygraves.

RODDY LLEWELLYN

The return of what I thought was one of my more valiant efforts at geometry was scarred by this note in the margin: 'I suggest you give up using this spider and buy a pen.'

GILES

I can only remember one comment from any of my school reports, which I thought rather splendid at the time and certainly fascinated my parents. One of my more observant masters wrote in the 'General Remarks' column: 'Very intelligent at times.'

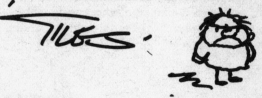

RONNIE BARKER

Report from Art Master: 'His work is encouraging at the moment – a little thin, but I'm sure he will expand a lot later on.'

BERYL REID

I went to a school of self-discipline – in fact you were never told *not* to do things. Once I fell out of a window and it took Miss Jenkin-Jones, the Headmistress, one hour to get me to own up that I must have been hanging out too far. I never did it again as it hurt and I got no sympathy, but it taught me to think for myself at an early age.

NORMAN WISDOM

I well remember the last report before my Army Education Course exam from a rather facetious Lance Corporal teacher: 'The boy is every inch a fool but luckily for him he's not very tall. Although I doubt any possibility of his ever being promoted, he may get sufficient marks to obtain his proficiency pay, and who knows, with a little bit of luck, he may perhaps, in time – about twenty-one years – get a pension!'

Norman Wisdom

GRAHAM

"You must not doodle on your exercise books!"

ARTHUR MARSHALL

I was very law-abiding and worked hard and my reports were usually quite good, though what the masters *ought* to have said about me was 'smug and complacent', for such I was. And some people would consider that I have remained so!

Arthur Marshall

ALAN PRICE

'The effort is there but the ability seems lacking.'

Alan Price

HARGREAVES

FREDERICK FORSYTH

For (mercifully) only two terms at school I was detailed to study the subject of physics and proved to be remarkably obtuse at it. While I could detect a certain weird logic in mathematics, some sense in trigonometry, a crossword-puzzle charm to geometry and even an oriental deviousness to alegbra, the laws of physics eluded me wholly.

Our master, a long-suffering gentleman by the name of Mr Stredder, who rejoiced in the unfortunate nickname of 'Belch', was concerned to persuade us to scatter iron filings on a sheet of white paper and then, by application and manoeuvring of magnets beneath the paper, to create 'magnetic fields' in visible plan layout. I was the only one in the class who could manipulate the magnets exactly as instructed and, in face of all the laws of physics, find my iron filings deposited unceremoniously on the floor.

At the end of the first term I achieved one mark in sixty for the exam, adjusted to 1½ per cent, the lowest ever recorded. After the second term Mr Stredder wrote in my report: 'This young man is trying – excessively trying.' We parted company with profuse and mutual expressions of relief.

Frederick Forsyth

ALEC GUINNESS

I can't remember any pertinent comments on
school reports other than the boring 'Could try
harder'. However, when I went before an
Admiralty Board during the '39–45 war there was
scribbled across my papers, 'Probably more to him
than meets the eye', to which another Admiral
added, 'There would need to be.'

Alec Guinness.

ROGER

If education is so important then why isn't it one of our subjects at school?

ROGER

REG SMYTHE

Mental arithmetic

I put my hand up –
and the teacher said:
'C'mon, now,
if Smythe knows
the answer,
everybody does.'

Reg Smythe

RICHARD STILGOE

'Unless he pulls his socks up, Richard will never
become a scientist.' C.W.P. (1958)
I didn't, so I haven't.

Richard Stilgoe (1981.)

NOELE GORDON

I hated every minute of it!

Noele Gordon

JOHN TIMPSON

I was sixteen and a half, struggling with 'A' level coordinate geometry and bored out of my mind. 'Timpson,' said my Form Master toward the end of the Easter term, 'it would appear that you are not learning anything from us – and we are certainly not learning anything from you.' So I made an excuse – and left. A month later I was working on the local paper, and I have never understood a word of coordinate geometry since . . .

EDWARD FOX

Reports which often said, 'Fox could do better if he tried', were irksome at the time, but in remembrance now seem to me a salutory comment very well worth remembering.

PAT PHOENIX

School days were the unhappiest, most miserable days of my life. The very thought of them sends shock waves of nausea through my brain, particularly when I think of the insensitive manner in which so many different personalities were, metaphorically, shovelled into the same mould!

CLIVE JENKINS

The report that sticks irritatingly in my mind is from my Gym Master: 'Needs this work.'

The other was my English mistress: 'Language too ornate.'

Clive Jenkins

DAVID STEEL

'*Physical Education*: He is quite hopeless but has a good sense of humour.'

David Steel

JUDI DENCH

'Judi would be a very good pupil if she *lived* in this world.'

SHIRLEY WILLIAMS

The only comment I can remember from my school report is, 'Should be more tidy', a comment doubtless many could still make!

SAM COSTA

Headmaster's comment

'I don't know how this school is going to get along without your son but from next term, we're going to try.'

Sam Costa

ED STEWART

'If he was as careful with his homework as he is with his pocket money, he would be an above-average pupil.'

Ed Stewart

LESLIE CROWTHER

I enjoyed my school days. Nottingham High School – walking to it along Forest Road in the autumn, looking for conkers, and swishing through the piles of fallen leaves. My nickname was Dormouse, as I was found asleep so often in class! This may have been a contributing factor when, years later, I was helping my daughter Caroline with her homework. I really worked hard to make it as accurate, informative, concise and imaginative as possible. It came back with a note in the margin from the teacher – 'Caroline, is this *really* your best work?'!

Leslie Crowther

ROY HUDD

'This boy has a rag-bag mind stuffed with information of no possible interest to anyone but himself.'

ANTONIA FRASER

My art report when I was eight read: 'Ideas good, execution faulty.'

(I gave it up.)

FFOLKES

KINGSLEY AMIS

My school was the most tolerant institution I have ever been part of. Everything since has been a let down.

Kingsley Amis

WARREN MITCHELL

Headmaster's report. Southgate County School, Palmers Green, London, c. 1941

'I cannot extend my usual congratulations to one who has come top of the form – the asterisk denotes why.'

★ *Detentions in term – 18.*

JOHN CRAVEN

My school report when I was about eight was summed up by the Headmaster, who wrote: 'He is keen and enthusiastic, but his brain works faster than his hands!'

And that is how it has always been!

LUCINDA PRIOR-PALMER

In 1963 my preparatory school reported under 'General' that I was 'inclined to be impertinent'. I had no idea what impertinent meant. My mother explained it to me and I remember fiery feelings of indignation, resolving that however naughty I might be, and however rebellious, I was *not* going to be thought of as cheeky ever again. I don't know whether or not I succeeded.

ERNIE WISE

Every time the teacher asked a question I was the first to raise my hand. By the time I got back, the question had been answered!

GEORGE MIKES

Our school reports in Hungary were different. They lacked those telling and memorable remarks. My dominant memory from school days is that we laughed and giggled all the time. Laughing was extremely dangerous and severely punished; that's why we found every silly and unfunny situation or slight mistake by a master irresistible. This was also a lesson for the future humourist: try to make good jokes when you can but, if you can't, make jokes on occasions when no one must laugh – and everyone will roar.

George Mikes

LORD SOPER

'This boy's writing has now sufficiently improved to enable us for the first time to see how really bad his work is.'

Donald Soper

BERYL BAINBRIDGE

'*English*: . . . though her written work is the product of an obviously lively imagination, it is a pity that her spelling derives from the same source.'

'*Geography*: Her knowledge of the subject is so poor as to make one wonder if she is simple-minded.'

Beryl Bainbridge

FRANKLIN

Got to know The Three R's 1939-45 REICH, RAIDS AND RUNNING.

FRANKLIN

MAC

Deputy Head's comment

'This student's examination papers are a disgrace. His Maths, Geography, Biology and History papers were particularly abysmal – liked the doodles around the edges though.'

DEREK NIMMO

I think perhaps the teacher who caused me the most misery was my Latin Master, one 'Fruity Williams'.

I was an *appalling* student and his great delight was to call upon me to decline my own name . . . 'Nimmo, Nimmas, Nimmat, etc. etc.' which he claimed was a verb meaning 'to be a nobody'!

PATRICK MOORE

Woodwork Master's comment

'During woodwork classes, wouldn't it be better if he went to the music room and played the piano quietly to himself?'

IAN CARMICHAEL

Housemaster's report, Bromsgrove School

'Ian will never make any progress with his
scholastic studies until he learns to concentrate on
his lessons and abandons his craving for negroid
music.'

LANCE PERCIVAL

Towards the end of my school career(!), I was
studying economics and at the end of term, my
parents were delighted to see that I came second in
the class. However, this lofty position was
somewhat lowered when the master involved
added the following: 'I feel I should point out that
there are only two boys in the school who take this
subject.'

THE EARL OF LICHFIELD

Although it did not apply to me, the following
report on French was written by a master at
Harrow School where I was educated: 'By the time
this boy learns French, he will be too old to cross
the Channel.'

EMLYN WILLIAMS

My teacher once wrote: 'You must concentrate entirely on your studies, and forget your ambition to waste time by mounting a school play.'

So my ambition had to be postponed!

Emlyn Williams

SIR LEONARD CHESHIRE

I remember at the age of ten not having finished my homework. On the way to school I sat on a bench, to put off the moment of arrival. A man came and sat down, and I thought:

'If only I were grown up and had no worries!'

Leonard Cheshire

LARRY

MICHAEL BOND

'Suffers from a distorted sense of humour!'

Michael Bond.

SUE LAWLEY

'*Physical Education:* I do believe Susan has glue in her plimsoles. *English:* Susan would do well not to distract her friends during class. If she applied a quarter of the effort she puts into clowning, to her work, I venture to say she could be quite brilliant.'

(Needless to say, I never did, so I'm not!)

STIRLING MOSS

I do not remember my school days as being great.
Quite frankly, the food was filthy, the masters
uninteresting and we were not allowed to talk to
girls.

SIR JOHN GIELGUD

Prep-school report on football
'Gielgud – an opportunist, merely.'

KATHERINE WHITEHORN

My best report story concerns my brother, John
Whitehorn, who used to work for the CBI.
During the war he was at Rugby, and his
housemaster had a very vivacious wife called
Peggy Thomas. They all played bridge in the
shelters in the evenings and at the end of a rather
pompous report containing remarks about
confirmation, the classics, etc., there was a brief
entry in red ink:
Bridge:
Plays his cards well but inclined to overbid. Peggy.

NICHOLAS PARSONS

When I was young I suffered from a stutter, which usually became worse under pressure. The effect of this situation made me stutter even more, which only infuriated my French master, till he said, 'I don't believe you really have a stutter, and I'm going to hit you with my cane every time you fluff on a word.' I still carry the scars to this day – not physical ones, since the swish of the cane did not hurt my buttocks very much – the real hurt was elsewhere. There are some, perhaps, who could say that I have to be grateful to that man, since it is significant that as the years passed, I managed to master – or control – my stutter, and have since gained a reputation for being able to speak clearly at some speed. On the other hand, this could just be that I was very keen to become an actor, and an actor with a stutter is not going to get very far!

Nicholas Parsons

KENNETH MORE
Victoria College, Jersey

The happiest memory of my school days was looking on the notice board on Wednesday afternoons and seeing that I had been chosen to play for the first eleven on the following Saturday at left half.

I felt ten feet tall, although I was only five feet eight!

BERNARD CRIBBINS

An abiding memory in these days of non-corporal punishment is of a lady teacher knocking seven bells out of a very large youth who had refused the strap and had taken a swing at the teacher! The whole class standing and cheering her on! Her left hook was a beauty.

Bernard Cribbins

RONNIE CORBETT

James Gillespie's School for Boys, Edinburgh, age nine

'Trying hard but talks too much.'

Ronnie Corbett

BILL TIDY

I didn't enjoy music at school, and used to forget my recorder deliberately.

On one occasion word got around that any boy without a recorder was in for it, so I hoped to pass in a crowd through the motions with a substitute! Sheer cheek saved me because although spotted, the teacher in question was magnanimous enough to reward enterprise with leniency.

FLORA ROBSON

In early days I went to morning school with the doctor's daughter. Children from the big houses were learning to read. We were all of different ages and sat around the dining-room table. I remember one small boy learning to read from *Reading Without Tears*. There was always a little picture above the world spelt out. C-A-T spelt out the little boy laboriously, and then looking at the picture triumphantly he murmured 'putty'.

Flora Robson

BARRY TOOK

I left school aged fifteen to no one's regret and years later at a school reunion of some kind (I may have even been a guest of honour, though I doubt it), my old Head Master, by then retired, said: 'Be honest, Took, you learned nothing here of any value at all, did you?'

Barry Took

ROBIN KNOX-JOHNSTON

My Maths Master once said to me:
'Knox-Johnston, if you ever go to sea, I am going to emigrate to Switzerland – by air.'

Robin Knox-Johnston

HENRY COOPER

I was never very good at school academically. I was always in trouble one way or another, and had the cane about three times a week. As the headmaster was about to cane me he always said: 'The one thing I like about you, Cooper, is that you always tell the truth.' But I always got the cane anyway, and I always wondered whether, if I had told a lie, I would have got out of it.

DAVID JACOBS

I think my happiest recollection of school was waking up in the morning that we were due to break up for the summer holidays. It was a morning and a moment that I always wanted to hold on to for as long as possible, but, alas, before I knew it had happened, I would be lying in bed on the morning that I was due to go back to school to start the winter term.

JUNE WHITFIELD

Maths report
'Always first with the answer but not always correct.'

ANTHONY DOWELL

One report that sticks in my mind was from my Form Master in which he called me a 'dilettante'. When this was explained to me, that I was like a 'butterfly that flitted from subject to subject without showing any signs of interest or knowledge of any', it only confirmed my original hatred of my Form Master!

COLLIN WHITTOCK

'Has worked well, though the results are mixed in quality . . .!'

BOB LANGLEY

'Langley's attitude always manages to imply that he could do much better if he only tried. I have come to the conclusion that this impression is deceiving. Not only is he incapable of doing better, but he would do well to devote his energies to those activities requiring physical, rather than mental exertion.'

Bob

MARK COX

Being substantial in my hindquarters as a youngster, at the ripe age of fifteen I was told I was going to be good at tennis because 'I had so much arse'!

CLIFF MICHELMORE

One moment I recall in particular from my school days was at the end of a lesson, at Cowes School, about molecules and atoms. The bell had gone and as we were about to leave, Mr Waller, the Science Master, said: 'Oh, I may leave you with this thought. For all of us know, we might be part of the molecular construction of a leg of a chair or a bit of coal in someone else's world and tonight we will end up on the fire. Good morning!'

ALAN COREN

Physics report

'Coren's grasp of elementary dynamics is truly astonishing. Had he lived in an earlier eon, I have little doubt but that the wheel would now be square and the principle of the lever just one more of man's impossible dreams.'

MELVYN BRAGG

My school reports are a very personal matter between my parents and myself. [JOKE.]

GLENDA JACKSON

The memory of school which springs most readily to mind is of me sitting in a locked cupboard. The rest of the class had conspired to hide the key and made what seemed to me ghostly rapping noises. All this happened throughout an English lesson. . . . No wonder I can't write!

Glenda Jackson

RICHARD BAKER

I was happy at school and depressingly acquiescent most of the time. I remember with gratitude even the rather hearty games master who gave me the slipper because I drew a cartoon of him drinking beer.

Richard Baker

JOHN INMAN

One day at school the Headmaster came into our classroom, pointed to me and said, 'Inman, you are the idiot who wants to be an actor. Go down to the Blackpool Repertory Theatre and you have a job.' I was thirteen then and that was my first appearance on the stage.

John Inman

AUBERON WAUGH

School is hell. My chief memories are of discomfort and terror. But the great advantage of a boarding school is that it prepares you for anything which might happen in the way of army life or prison. Prison can have no terrors after the compulsory games, forced church attendances and revolting food of school, and the army was like a holiday camp. My school reports from Downside used to arrive in a folder, and it seemed an act of common prudence to steam it open before my parents had a chance to study some of the more austere comments contained. As a result, I even now possess some of the originals and can read them over if I choose, in my quieter moments. They are very rude indeed.

Auberon Waugh

JANET BROWN
At the age of twelve attempting to sing in front of an adjudicator and shaking so badly that hardly a note would come out, I was told to go and sit down as it sounded 'like sliding up and down a greasy pole'!

Janet Brown

DELIA SMITH
Autumn Term, 1953
'Delia talks too hard and works too little.'

Delia

LAURIE LEE

I had a violin but no bow, but I was very keen to learn the instrument. So I used to go along to the lesson and hum. In my report, under 'Music', the master wrote: 'Lack of bow has spoilt his chances, but think he will do well.'

Laurie Lee

ARTHUR LOWE

Sooner or later, every teacher would inevitably say: 'You *stupid* boy!'

Arthur Lowe

P. D. JAMES

I remember the excitement of winning the short-story prize. My story was highly dramatic and exciting, and featured, I remember, a cynical and handsome hero, a desert island and a plane crash. It ended with the words: '. . . and then his fingers tightened round the hypodermic.' So perhaps I was even then fascinated by mystery and death. My prize was a copy of the *Oxford Book of English Verse*. I still have it, but the story, alas, is lost even from memory.

P. D. James

JAKE THACKRAY

I went to a Catholic grammar school in the north where, one year, the fathers agreed to give us (informally) obverse-side reports.
Of Thackray, J., they said:

Fakryz yoos of langwidj zinfexus	ENGLISH
Should go very far. Please	MATHS
Is trying.	HISTORY
Thracray longa. Vita brevis.	LATIN
May he rot in heaven.	R.E.

J. Thackray.

DEBORAH KERR

A brief comment that sums up my memories of school days: 'HELL'!

Deborah Kerr

JOE GORMLEY

The one significant episode I can remember is when studying to try to pass the examination which would qualify me to go to grammar school, when I inadvertently overheard my parents saying it would be impossible financially, if I should pass. I did not take the examination and the Headmaster said to me afterwards, when no one had passed, 'Gormley, you would have walked it.'

Joe Gormley

TONY HART

An early recollection of what I considered harsh
disciplinary action occurred when, as a new
resident chorister in a West End church, I was
found to be giggling during the psalm that goes:
'Like as the hart desireth the water brooks . . . .'.
Retribution came after evensong. In the words of
the Psalter, 'He smiteth his enemy in his hinder
parts and put him to a perpetual shame.' Glad to
say the same has now left me – just.

REV. DAVID SHEPPARD

When I was ten years old my headmaster wrote about my bowling: 'Young Sheppard, unless I am very much mistaken, will one day cause a lot of batsmen a great deal of trouble with his left-arm slows.' He was very much mistaken! I was never such a good bowler as when I was ten.

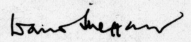

LES DAWSON

My teacher – an august, grey, iron sort of scholar – looked upon my school work rather in the manner of a scientist when faced with a wart.

To sum up my dreary years, the phrase my teacher adopted will describe fully my academic worth.

'Dawson,' he said gravely, 'I have in my time taught near idiots and imbeciles, but for sheer progressive asininity you are quite beyond recall in the spectrum of knowledge.'

DERYCK GUYLER

'Your writing, Guyler, resembles a drunken spider doing the Charleston, with a headache.'

'Your Maths paper has been marked out of two hundred. I award you two marks for sheer ingenuity, because never in my life have I seen so many figures which have meant absolutely nothing.'

43

DAVID DIMBLEBY

Housemaster at Charterhouse, 1955

'He has a great deal of energy and is an ebullient member of the House, sometimes excessively. He must keep an eye on this ebullience. It can be overdone.'

BARRY SHEENE

'Barry must realize that the world does not revolve around motor cycles, and thinking it does will not earn him a living.'

ARTHUR ASKEY

I must have been one of the first vandals – I carved my initials (A.A.) on my desk. The first time I met Paul McCartney, he said he had sat at the same desk which he and the rest of the form regarded as a sort of shrine because the great A.A. had sat there.

I won the egg-gathering race at the school sports in 1916 (and still have the medal). That's the race where eggs are spaced out about every ten yards and you have to gather them, place them in your school cap, and then dash for the next one until they are all safely gathered up. I was preening myself on my victory in this event, when the Sports Master said to me: 'And so you *should* have won it. You are nearer to the ground than any of the other boys.'

PAUL DANIELS

I remember getting six per cent in an annual Latin examination, and it being the highest mark! And spending many French lessons doing magic tricks for the French tutor who was fascinated by them. (He was Polish by birth, French by education and English by choice – what a sensible fellow.) All that rubbish they feed you about 'school days are the best days of your life' is codswallop – it's *marvellous* when you leave so long as you don't grow up!

JIMMY SAVILLE

My school (an elementary one) was the best.
It taught me the Four 'Rs'.
Reading
Righting (!)
Reckoning Up
Right & Rong (!!)
and that was quite enough for a survivor like me.

LORD ROBENS OF WALDINGHAM

Form Master, 1926

'This boy has tremendous potential if he would
only apply himself. He spends a lot of time arguing
about current affairs with teachers and pupils.
Perhaps he is destined to be a politician.'

MAGNUS PYKE

If there had been an Examinations are Fun Society
when I was at school, I should have been a
member. There is a good deal more fun to be had
from guessing what questions are going to be
asked and concocting the kind of answers the
examiners would like to be given (whether they
are right or not) than in breaking one's fingernails
at cricket.

BARBARA DICKSON
Music teacher at Woodmill School, Dunfermline
'Well Barbara, you may be not the best singer in
the school, but you're certainly the loudest!'

Barbara Dickson

BARRY CRYER

My very last school report read: 'He must learn that glibness is no substitute for knowledge.'

(I immediately made a vow that one day I would make a living out of glibness!)

I decided that adopting the role of a junior Bilko was the key to survival at school. Two ventures spring to mind: a black market in lunch tickets – shameful, but highly profitable and resulting in a beating; and selling the short cut to the cross-country run in a sealed envelope for 6d. This last scheme collapsed when I discovered other entrepreneurs, who had bought it from me, selling it for 4d.

GEOFF LAWS

SARAH GREENE

Games report

'Sarah must learn that vivacity is *not* a substitute for *hard work*.'

Sarah Greene

LEN DEIGHTON

My most vivid memory of school is of a boy saying to me, 'Deighton, I've been thinking, and every boy in the class is either good at sport or good at lessons. You are the only one who is no good at either.'

It must be emphasized that his tone and manner were purely scientific and without malice. We both thought about this interesting problem for a long time without figuring out why my deplorable state had come about.

Len Deighton

BRIAN REDHEAD

English Lit. report, summer, 1945

'Redhead is prone to idle effusion.'

Brian Redhead

BASIL BOOTHROYD

'His goalkeeping is more dramatic than successful.'

JILLY COOPER

'Jilly has set herself an extremely low standard which she has failed to maintain.'

JOHN MILLS

Maths report, Norwich High School, 1921

'Mills lacks concentration – spends most of the time gazing out of the window and dreaming.'
    Perfectly correct. I was even then dreaming of the theatre!

KENNETH WILLIAMS

'Quick to grasp the bones of a subject: slow to develop' – which I thought made me sound like an inefficient osteopath.

DENISE ROBINS

I was always the leading light in any school plays. Once I had to pretend to be in a fire which I couldn't put out, and I acted this so realistically that the Reverend Mother sent up a message to the stage to say that 'Denise should calm down.'

TIP-A-TAP!
TIP-A-TAP!
TIP-A-TAP!

SANDY WILSON

I didn't care much for my prep school: the food was vile, and the discipline very repressive. But the teaching standard was very high. One day, when my attention was wandering, the Latin Master said 'The trouble with you, Wilson, is that you spend all your time thinking about John Gilbert and Greta Garbo.' He was right – but out of date. It was 1937, and I was thinking about Fred Astaire and Ginger Rogers.

Sandy Wilson

ROWAN ATKINSON
Headmaster's report
'This boy is bone idle.'

WILLIAM WHITELAW
'He can do good work when he wants to, but, alas, such occasions are rare.'

CATHERINE COOKSON

Miss Nesbit of Simonside School, Tyne Dock, was a beloved teacher in the days prior to the First World War until she exposed me as a liar.

It must have come to her ears that I was always bragging about having horses, cars and servants. After having chosen the children to take part in the Christmas concert, she mentioned that they had a sledge but no horn for Father Christmas to honk, and so, perhaps, Katie would loan them one from her cars.

Oh dear! The pangs of childhood!

Catherine Cookson.

RAYMOND BAXTER

Form VA, Ilford County High School, 1938

'If he would apply to his work the energy and enthusiasm he devotes to his many other interests, he could yet do well.'

If only I had . . . who knows?

Raymond Baxter

RON GREENWOOD

Most of my school reports were related to the fact that if only I had spent more time on the academic side and less time thinking about football, I would be a greater success in life.

Ron Greenwood

ART BUCHWALD

I was the class clown and always tried to break the other kids up. I guess I started my career in public school trying to make people laugh. The teachers didn't think I was *that* funny but I did all right with the rest of the audience.

Art Buchwald

DIANA RIGG
Matron's report, St Christopher's, Little Missenden, c.1946
'Diana has been very tiresome in the dormitory this term.'

LORD WILLIS OF CHISLEHURST

When I was leaving school at the age of fourteen, I had a two-second 'career interview' with my Headmaster, a certain Mr Pinchbeck. He was rather like his name. He asked me what I wished to do for the future and I told him that I intended to become a writer. His response was a cackle followed by the remark: 'You will never make a writer in a hundred years. You haven't got the imagination for it or the intelligence. Go away and learn a good trade.'

SIR HARRY SECOMBE

Headmaster's report, Easter, 1936

Secombe, H. 14 years, 6 months. 5'. 6 stone 11½ lbs.

   'A very disappointing result from a capable lad. There must be a greater striving for *accuracy*.'

   He must have been referring to the mark of 0 per cent in geometry.

ROD HULL

Headmaster, Sheerness Technical School

'Hull, I don't know what's going to become of you.'

DAVID LANGDON

At school there was always one fringe subject which pupils used as an excuse to release all their pent-up frustrations. Art was one such, sadly for me as it was my favourite period. Our Art Master, F. P. Brown, a gentle bearded giant of a man, was curiously slow to anger and was hence put upon unmercifully. On rare occasions, when the provocation was unbearable, he could hurl a miscreant bodily down the flight of stone steps leading from the art class.

Imprinted on my memory is the day when he was seated next to a boy helping him with a drawing. Normally I too would be engrossed in my own work, but I found myself in his defence remonstrating with a particularly unruly mob in the back row. Wrestling with them on the floor, I looked up in horror to find our Art Master gazing down at me.

'Oh no!' he said, with a look of such abject pain and disappointment that it is still etched on my mind, 'Not you too, Langdon.'

David Langdon

TOM JACKSON

Each day I was set the task of reading the leading article in the *Yorkshire Post* and looking up any word I did not know. It was boring work but did wonders for my vocabulary.

Tom Jackson

HARRY CARPENTER

I recall vividly being categorized by the chap who took us for gym (they presumably call it P.T. or P.E. today) as 'inattentive' and 'inclined to be lazy'. I suppose that is what has given me my present deep insight into all forms of sporting activity.

JIMMY EDWARDS

St Paul's Cathedral Choristers' Magazine, c. 1934

'*Cricket*: A player of great bonhomie.
Convulsed with laughter when bowled . . .
usually for a duck.'

CYRIL SMITH

'This boy would be a better scholar if he had less to
say!'

JEFFREY ARCHER

Wellington School, 1955, age fifteen

'*English*: Archer's essays always make me feel he is destined to be a great story teller or a politician.'

But my own comments on education are summed up by my entry in *Who's Who*.

'*Education*: By my wife since leaving Wellington School and Brasenose College, Oxford.'

And my wife received the following report at school:

'MARY ARCHER (née WEEDEN)
Cheltenham Ladies College, 1956. Age eleven.

History	....	1st
French	....	1st
Latin	....	1st
Maths	....	1st
English	....	1st
Geography	....	1st
Divinity	....	1st
Needlework	....	2nd

Needlework report
Mary mustn't cry when she comes second.'
Mary went on to gain a First-Class Honours degree from Oxford in Chemistry and since we have been married has done no needlework.

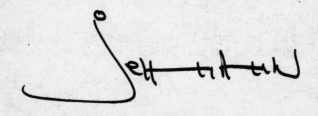

59

JAMES HERRIOT

'His mathematics marks remain very low but his English essays show that he has a feeling for words.'

James Herriot

ROBERT ROBINSON

One of the masters at my school felt no need to temper truth with civility. On one boy's report – I should love to claim it was mine, but it wasn't – he was particularly succinct. He simply wrote: 'Eats, and cheats.'

Robert Robinson

ERIC MORCAMBE

Teacher to Eric's mother

'Mrs Bartholomew, I hate to say this, but your Eric will never get anywhere in life.'

Eric Morcambe OB DR. LITT.

DAVID BAILEY

'Hopeless, but possibilities if he'd show interest in anything.'

IAN WALLACE

Kindergarten report, c. 1927

'*Form:* Ian is lazy, inattentive and talks too much.
Gardening: Frequently wishes to change his job.
Singing: Good.'

TERRY SCOTT

Report on performance in school play

'O. J. Scott playing Macbeth did well, but would
have done better if he had really known not just the
words – but what they meant.'

Terry Scott

RICHARD BRIERS

Headmaster's report

'It would seem that Briers thinks he is running the school and not me. If this attitude persists one of us will have to leave.'

PETE MURRAY

My school reports were generally horrific. One master even suggested that 'the way things are going, he would be lucky to get a job as a cloakroom attendant!' How right he was!

Pete Murray

BOB PAISLEY

I have vivid memories of the woodwork lesson and the Master who went with it. The weekly lesson always began in the same way. Each pupil produced his individual work while the Master pronounced judgement on the exercise. The best model was always highly praised and it was always made by the same boy. When my turn came to make the long walk to the back of the room with my effort the humiliation always ended with the word 'disgraceful'.

It was arranged one week that I should take up the model made by the expert woodworker. As I stood confidently expecting at least nine out of ten, the rest of the class fell about when the dreaded words were uttered: 'Paisley, this is disgraceful.'

Bob

ENOCH POWELL

It must have been in 1927 that Mr Sheldon, Form Master of the Lower Sixth at King Edwards School, Birmingham, addressed me in class as follows: 'Powell, you will not go up to Oxford, for two reasons: you cannot write an English essay and a combination of you and Balliol would be intolerable. You will instead go up to Cambridge and write one of your Latin proses, which will win you a major open scholarship at Trinity.' What a wise man he was!

JOHN ARLOTT

Perhaps the most significant comment I recall from my schooldays in a country grammar school where the normal currency was fisticuffs between the boys and flogging by the staff – the nearest one could come to greeny-yallery was to be caught reading *The Times Literary Supplement* – was when the English master said to me, looking up from the essay he was correcting, 'Why don't you stop trying to write this fine English, Arlott – you will never be able to.' How right he was!

JOHN LE CARRÉ

My prep school reports complained that I was idle and unpopular and cowardly in games. My public school reports complained that I was unhappy. In the aggregate, the reports were witless and illiterate and unhelpful: a perfect preparation, in fact, for being reviewed by English critics!

John le Carré

MARY WHITEHOUSE

When I came to leave school the very 'proper' headmistress whose life I had made something of a burden with my antics said she would find it very difficult to write a helpful testimonial for me! 'However,' she said, 'if you'll write one for yourself, Mary, I'll consider signing it.' Which I did and she did! It didn't strike me at the time, but it has many times since, that underneath her very forbidding exterior she had a sense of humour.

FRANK TOPPING

English report

'Keep up your imaginative writing. I think you might have a way with words.'

DAVID KOSSOFF

'David should try to work harder at subjects that do not interest him as much as art and handwork. He might argue less and listen more. He should try to give up his position as class comedian. He is unlikely to succeed as an actor.'

David Kossoff

PETER JONES

I was about eight or nine when I moved up from the prep school to Wem Grammar School. I was very keen to be an athlete and when entries were invited for the annual sports, I put my name down for everything. On the great day I found myself in the 'mile' which was really a senior boys' event. I was soon lapped by the other runners and the race was over while I still had a lap to do. But I didn't drop out – with the result that I got a big hand from the crowd at the finishing line. Next day, at school prayers, the Headmaster mentioned the incident and praised my 'grit' and 'pluck' and so forth. And he presented me with a little silver cup about two inches high. I have it still and when I feel like giving up on something I try hard to find that bit extra which will help me to finish. I believe that Headmaster's gesture has made a real difference to my whole life.

Peter Jones

JEAN ROOK

The Maths Master, on passing her 'O' level maths exam

'All I can say is that it was the easiest set of papers in fifteen years, and you still didn't deserve it.'

Jean Rook

ALAN AYCKBOURN

The only comment I remember clearly from my school report was one made by my Housemaster at Hailebury when I was fifteen. It read 'altogether too flamboyant in manner and appearance' – which at fifteen I was rather proud of!

ROBIN COUSINS

'Robin's compositions this year have been most enlightening. It hasn't mattered what subject he has been given to write about he has somehow managed to give me a lesson on the art of ice-skating.'

CHRISTINA FOYLE

Headmistress' report

'Christina is incapable of concentration and sustained effort. She will always be a butterfly, flitting from flower to flower.' (I have run my luncheons for fifty years.)

BILL ODDIE
Headmaster's report at the age of ten
'Would do well to adopt a more adult attitude. . . .'
Thank God I didn't!

[signature: Bill Oddie]

TERRY WOGAN
Kindergarten report
'If we could just find some way to stop Terry from
running away, we might be able to beat some
learning into him.'

LAWRIE McMENEMY

One of my teachers was an elderly, popular man who, for starters, insisted that Hitler was not dead but was, in fact, thriving in Ireland. His main passion was cricket, and many was the time, as he walked in to start a lesson, that a tennis ball would mysteriously roll from the back of the class to the front. He would then say, if in the right mood, 'What is this? Could it possibly be a ball?' Someone would then have to reply, 'I think it is a ball, Sir.' He would then ask for it to be thrown to him as hard as the boy wanted. Inadvertently, of course, it would strike him and fly off in all directions. He would then start to demonstrate his off-spinners, leg-spinners and his famous googly. By this time, if we had played our cards right, the lesson would be over!

JIM DAVIDSON

French teacher, St Auston's, Charlton

'Davidson. You will never be famous as long as you've got a hole under your nose!'

GEOFF BOYCOTT

I enjoyed my school days very much indeed – they were a pleasure – I loved every one of them.

2 SUMS RIGHT OUT OF EIGHT ... SIX OF THE BEST ON THE BACKSIDE!

ROLF HARRIS

The occasion gave me great prestige – showing off the bruises to all and sundry. Mum spoilt it all by getting into a rage and complaining to the Headmaster.

JOAN COLLINS

Final report from RADA

'With so much in her favour the student is hampered by the weakness of her voice. She seems to lack the confidence to project and make the most of the voice she does possess.

'If she will make up her mind to cast away fear, doubt and self-consciousness, she will find her confidence increasing, and the unsure element in her acting will disappear.

'Otherwise it will be "the films" for her, and that would be such a pity!'

DAVID BELLAMY

School testimonial

'Bellamy is a good fellow, is maturing well but is academically useless.'

MIKE YARWOOD

Being able to 'take people off' started at a very early age for me. I always seemed to have the ability to catch the voice and mannerisms of those with whom I came into contact.

It made me quite popular with my family and my school friends, but sometimes not so popular with others. Among the latter were teachers at the last school I attended. Without consciously thinking about it, I found it quite easy to 'take off' most of them; all teachers have over-emphasised mannerisms, and these were no exceptions. I was quite sure that, when it was not happening to them, a lot of the teachers were quite chuffed with my ability to impersonate their colleagues, and even some of the biggest mischief-makers among the pupils. My belief was borne out when it came time for me to leave the school. There was a little do at which all the school-leavers gathered, and the teachers insisted that I did my impressions of the staff. Each time there was loud laughter, but I noticed that the victim in each case stayed strangely silent.

BIDDY BAXTER

'Biddy has worked very well during the term and her year's work has been very satisfactory. She shows interest in all that she does and she is a very cheery little girl with very pleasant manners.'

DR BENJAMIN SPOCK

My grades wobbled from high to low all the way from first grade through medical school. I enjoyed a few teachers and hated a few sadists who threatened the class with failure and made my mouth so dry with anxiety that I couldn't swallow my sandwich.

Ben Spock

FIONA FULLERTON

From the Principal, Elmhurst Ballet School

Fiona unfortunately mistook laburnum seeds for garden peas when in the garden the other day, and swallowed some. No harm was done as she and another child, who had done the same thing, were taken straight to hospital and given a stomach wash out (laburnum seeds can cause very nasty symptoms of poisoning). Fiona is none the worse, but the incident took ten years off my life at the time!'

ROBERT POWELL

In the space left for 'High Master's Remarks' on my last report from Manchester Grammar School, all he could think of to say was: 'Very much enjoyed his King Lear'. So much for eight years of a classical education!

Robert Powell

THELWELL N.   Upper III A

This spelling is atrosijus.

N. Thelwell.

MARTIN JARVIS
- *Mathematics:* Fair
- *History:* Fair
- *Geography:* Fair
- *Physics:* Very Fair
- *Chemistry:* Only Fair
- *Latin:* Fair

Headmaster's comment: A good all-round record!

Martin · Jarvis ·

K9

UPDATE RETEST EX-GALLIFREY
ACADEMY ROBOT ASSESSMENT CENTRE

SUBJECT: K9

DESIGNER: Professor Marius, Earth

IMPROVEMENTS: Theta Sigma Mk
(Codename: Doctor) et alii

INTERIM PROGRESS REPORT:

BEHAVIOUR: Lamentable. We can only suppose
that K9 has suffered circuit exposure and
inadvertent conditioning through contact with
earthbeings and other primitives. Tests indicate
severe anthropomorphism, to wit, pigheadedness,
predisposition to independent action and lack of
respect for established Gallifrey Academy modes
of conduct.

CONCLUSION: K9 has shown great promise but
less judgement than we would desire. In particular,
he should curb his altruistic impulses and stop
saving people at such risk to himself. It is futile to
say that he *can do better* – although he could and
should – since we have seen from his exploits in the
future that he doesn't. His tendency towards
heroics and self-sacrifice, plus his emotive
responses, such as loyalty, irritability and
increasing signs of affection (not programmed but
learned) lead us to the regrettable conclusion that
he is not the credit to the Academy that we hoped.

SUBJECT'S COMMENTS: Big words from tiny
minds. Report negative, therefore ignored and
shredded. K9.

A. J. WENTWORTH, BA

H. F. Ellis

'One of the funniest books ever . . . it deserves to follow *The Henry Root Letters* to the top of the bestsellers' *Sunday Express*

There is chalk in his fingernails and paper darts fill the air as A. J. Wentworth, BA, mathematics master at Burgrove Preparatory School, unwittingly opens the doors that lead not to knowledge but to chaos and confusion. Here are his collected papers in which you can at last discover the truth about the fishing incident in the boot room, the real story about the theft of the headmaster's potted plant, and even the answer to the sensitive question of whether or not Mr Wentworth was trying to have carnal knowledge of matron on that one, memorable occasion.

'I did indeed laugh aloud till I cried' *Graham Lord, Sunday Express*

'A book of such hilarious nature that I had to give up reading it in public as my shrieks were causing both surprise and annoyance to those present' *Arthur Marshall, New Statesman*

'Few books have made me laugh out loud quite so often' *Christopher Matthew, Evening Standard*

£1.25

THE BOOK OF DAYS

Bob Monkhouse

Take a day-by-day look at some of the more outrageous and unusual events of history through the eyes of one of TV's zaniest personalities, Bob Monkhouse.

Remember these red letter days:

2nd November
This is the birthday of the world's first test tube baby rabbit! The bunny-under-glass was presented to the New York Academy of Medicine today . . . in 1939. I wouldn't have thought rabbits needed any artificial help with that sort of thing.

19th September
False teeth were first advertised for sale today in America in 1768 by a goldsmith named Paul Revere, born – are you ready for this? – in Massachusetts!

24th June
The Battle of Bannockburn took place in 1314. Sir Harry Lauder said, 'The British dispersed the Scottish army with an underhand trick. They passed the hat around.'

11th July
Two totally blind soccer teams played to a 2–2 tie in Lima, Peru, today in 1973 . . . using a sonic ball and a handful of dried peas.

£1.75

BESTSELLERS FROM ARROW

All these books are available from your bookshop or newsagent or you can order them direct. Just tick the titles you want and complete the form below.

A CHOICE OF CATASTROPHIES	Isaac Asimov	£1.95
BRUACH BLEND	Lillian Beckwith	95p
THE HISTORY MAN	Malcolm Bradbury	£1.60
A LITTLE ZIT ON THE SIDE	Jasper Carrott	£1.25
EENY MEENY MINEY MOLE	Marcel A'Agneau	£1.50
HERO	Leslie Deane	£1.75
TRAVELS WITH FORTUNE	Christine Dodwell	£1.50
11th ARROW BOOK OF CROSSWORDS	Frank Henchard	95p
THE LOW CALORIE MENU BOOK	Joyce Hughes	90p
THE PALMISTRY OF LOVE	David Brandon-Jones	£1.50
DEATH DREAMS	William Katz	£1.25
PASSAGE TO MUTINY	Alexander Kent	£1.50
HEARTSOUNDS	Marth Weinman Lear	£1.75
LOOSELY ENGAGED	Christopher Matthew	£1.25
HARLOT	Margaret Pemberton	£1.60
TALES FROM A LONG ROOM	Peter Tinniswood	£1.50
INCIDENT ON ATH	E. C. Tubb	£1.15
THE SECOND LADY	Irving Wallace	£1.75
STAND BY YOUR MAN	Tammy Wynette	£1.75
DEATH ON ACCOUNT	Margaret Yorke	£1.00

Postage

Total

ARROW BOOKS, BOOKSERVICE BY POST, PO BOX 29, DOUGLAS, ISLE OF MAN, BRITISH ISLES

Please enclose a cheque or postal order made out to Arrow Books Limited for the amount due including 10p per book for postage and packing for orders within the UK and 12p for overseas orders.

Please print clearly

NAME ....

ADDRESS...

....

Whilst every effort is made to keep prices down and to keep popular books in print, Arrow Books cannot guarantee that prices will be the same as those advertised here or that the books will be available.